m nday
morning®

Writing Hangups

D1378445

By Murray Suid

Illustrated by Lisa Levine

This book is for John and Peggy Woodworth

Publisher: Roberta Suid
Editor: Mary McClellan
Design: David Hale
Production: Susan Pinkerton

Other books by the author: *Book Factory, Editing, Greeting Cards, Letter Writing, Research, Sentences, Speaking and Listening, Stories, Words*

Entire contents copyright © 1988 by Monday Morning Books, Inc., Box 1680, Palo Alto, California 94302

Monday Morning is a registered trademark of Monday Morning Books, Inc.

ISBN 0-912107-73-1

Printed in the United States of America
9 8 7 6 5 4 3 2

CONTENTS

INTRODUCTION

Children—like adults—sometimes write for themselves. More often, they want to share their words. *Writing Hangups* is about such sharing.

BEYOND NOTEBOOK PAPER

If you want kids to publish their ideas far and wide, be willing to go beyond notebook-size paper. Try banners, bumper stickers, buttons, posters, wearable words, and other "real world" formats frequently used by business people, poets, politicians, and—yes—teachers.

The dozens of projects you'll find in *Writing Hangups* aim to get children's writing seen, read, talked about, enjoyed, used, and celebrated. You can accomplish this feat by putting their words on the wall, in the air, everywhere. This approach will enable your young writers to find multitudes of readers at home, around the school, and throughout the community.

WHAT YOU'LL NEED

The main ingredient in making eye-catching Writing Hangups is something every kid has plenty of: imagination. Of course, imagination needs stuff to work with. The projects presented in the following pages use inexpensive materials such as yarn, foil, balloons, clothespins, bottle caps, and glue. If you have a word processor that can print giant letters, you'll find plenty of uses for it.

One key material is scratch paper for making rough drafts of the text that will appear in the Hangups. By refining their thoughts, children will get important practice in the vital composition skill of editing.

SHORT BUT GOOD

Most Writing Hangups use only a few words, whether in the form of a sentence, a rhyme, or a mini-essay. The emphasis is on quality, not quantity. Rewriting a bumper sticker sentence four or five times—to get every syllable just right—may offer more skill building than cranking out a three-page story.

In other words...

LESS IS MORE

BALLOON-O-GRAM

MATERIALS: balloons, felt-tip pen, string, tape

DIRECTIONS:
1. Make up a one-word message. It could be a party announcement or the title of a bulletin board.
2. Blow up one balloon for each letter of the message.
3. Write one letter of the word on each balloon.
4. Tie a string around the end of each balloon.
5. Attach the balloons to a door, wall, or long piece of string.

BANNER BANTER

MATERIALS: paper, writing tools, chalk, old white sheet, wide-tip markers, hole punch or scissors, string or yarn

DIRECTIONS:
1. Think up a message that should be hung out a window or from a ceiling: for example, news about a play or concert.
2. Use the chalk to print the words lightly on the sheet. Make sure the letters are big enough to be read from a distance.
3. Go over the letters using the markers. To make the banner a real eye-catcher, use a different color for the most important word, or start each word with a different color.
4. Punch or cut holes in the upper corners.
5. Pass the string or yarn through the holes, and hang the banner.

BODY BIOGRAPHY

MATERIALS: butcher paper, writing tools, scissors, thumbtack or hole punch and string

DIRECTIONS:
1. Have someone lie down on a large piece of butcher paper. Using a pencil, trace around the person to make an outline.
2. Cut out the figure.
3. Think up all sorts of things to say about the person.
4. Write the words all over the character. Put dreams, memories, and other thoughts in the head. If the person is good at soccer or kick ball, write that fact in the foot.
5. Use a thumbtack to display the paper person on a bulletin board. Or, with a hole punch, make a hole at the top of the head and dangle the figure from a piece of string.

Variation 1: Glue a picture of a famous person's face onto the head and fill the figure with facts about that person.

Variation 2: Instead of a person, use the shape of a real animal or a character like Mickey Mouse.

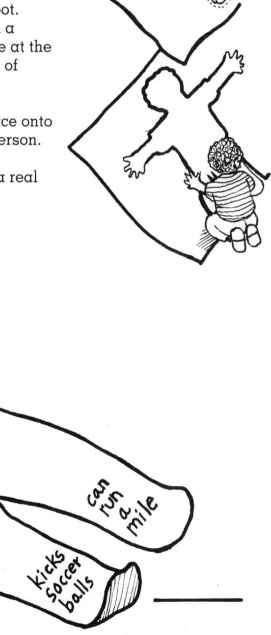

BOXY BOOK

MATERIALS: shoe box, envelope box or cardboard carton (with top), plain paper to cover the box, writing tools, glue, objects related to the story and small enough to fit into the box

DIRECTIONS:

1. Think up a story or a report that has five or six scenes or chapters.
2. Cut a piece of paper to fit over each side of the box.
3. Write the material for each "page" of the boxy book. Be sure to number the pages.
4. Glue the pages onto the box.
5. For each page or scene, include an object or picture inside the box. Each page should end by inviting the readers to look inside and find the object.

Variation: Instead of a story, use a riddle. Put one clue to the riddle on each side of the box. Put the answer to the riddle inside the box.

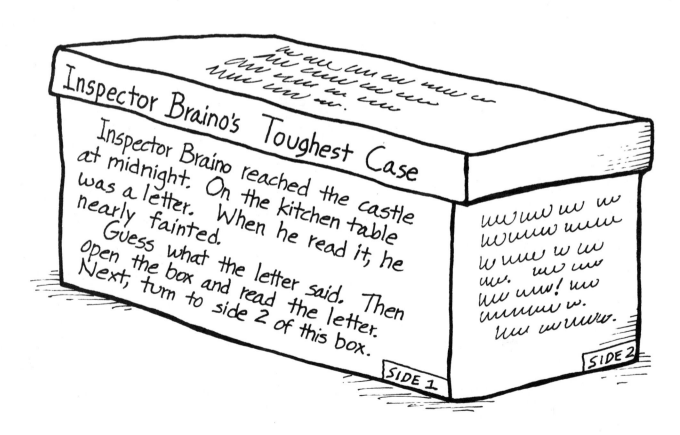

BUMPER STICKER

MATERIALS: paper, writing tools, white self-sticking shelf paper, permanent markers

DIRECTIONS:
1. Think up a subject for a bumper sticker. A bumper sticker can be about school, pets, clubs, hobbies, or almost anything.
2. Practice writing the message. It should have no more than eight words. Short messages are easier to read.
3. With a pencil, lightly print the message on a piece of the shelf paper. Make the letters big enough to read from a distance.
4. When the spacing looks right, go over the letters using one or more permanent markers.
5. Get permission to attach the bumper sticker to someone's car.

BUS BILLBOARD

MATERIALS: paper, writing tools

DIRECTIONS:
1. Find out if the local bus company or the school board will post public service announcements in their buses. If yes, get the exact measurements for the poster and the kind of paper it must be printed on.
2. Think up a message of interest to riders: for example, ways to support the schools.
3. Print the message on the poster paper. Add a picture.
4. Deliver the poster to the bus company.

BUTTON BULLETIN

MATERIALS: paper, writing tools, construction paper, jar lid, scissors, colored markers, drawing or photo (optional), glue, glitter, pin or masking tape

DIRECTIONS:
1. Think up a short message containing five or fewer words. It could be about a favorite thing or about someone who is running for office.
2. Draw the shape of the button on the construction paper. For a circle, trace around a jar lid.
3. Cut the button out.
4. First letter the message lightly in pencil. When the spacing looks right, go over the letters in ink. To grab attention, use different colors for different words or letters. Try adding a picture or photo.
5. For a sparkling look, dab on some glue and sprinkle on some glitter.
6. Use a pin or masking tape to attach the button.

CALENDAR CHRONICLE

MATERIALS: paper, writing tools, calendar page, thumbtack or tape, folder or binder

DIRECTIONS:
1. Make a blank calendar page. Use a calendar for a model.
2. Label the calendar with the name of the month and the name of the person whose calendar it is.
3. At the top, draw a picture. For example, a picnic scene might be just right for July.
4. Find out what day the month begins: for example, Tuesday. Then number the days.
5. Post the calendar using a thumbtack or tape.
6. In each day's box, write a word or sentence that tells something important or unusual that happened.
7. At the end of the year, make a book of the filled-in pages.

Variation: Keep a calendar for someone else: for example, a younger brother, a pet, or even a make-believe character.

SUNDAY	MONDAY	TUESDAY	WEDNESDAY
1 Flew to Paris. Kept the Eiffel Tower from falling down.	**2** Saved dog trapped in a gold mine.	**3** Used super breath to blow out a forest fire.	**4**

CAN OF WORDS

MATERIALS: paper, writing tools, tin can, scissors, glue

DIRECTIONS:
1. Write a story, poem, report, or riddle.
2. Remove the label from the can.
3. Cut a piece of paper large enough to wrap around the can. This will be the new label.
4. On a piece of scratch paper, write a short advertisement about the story, report, poem, or riddle that will be placed in the can.
5. Copy the advertisement onto the label. Add a picture that gives a hint about the piece of writing that will go in the can.
6. Glue the label to the can.
7. Roll up the piece of writing, and put it in the can.

CAP CAPTION

MATERIALS: plain (unlettered) cap, colored felt, needle and thread

DIRECTIONS:
1. Think up a short message for the cap. It could be to cheer on a favorite team or it could be about a chore.
2. Cut out felt letters to spell the message.
3. Sew the letters onto the cap.

CHAIN LETTER

MATERIALS: paper, writing tools, colored paper, glue

DIRECTIONS:
1. Write a letter on scratch paper.
2. Cut the colored paper into strips.
3. On each strip, write a sentence from the letter.
4. Make a loop out of the first strip, with the writing on the outside. Glue the ends together.
5. Loop the second strip inside the first and glue it.
6. Continue adding loops until all the strips have been added to the chain. Then hang the chain letter where the person it's meant for will find it.

Variation: Make a chain story or a chain poem.

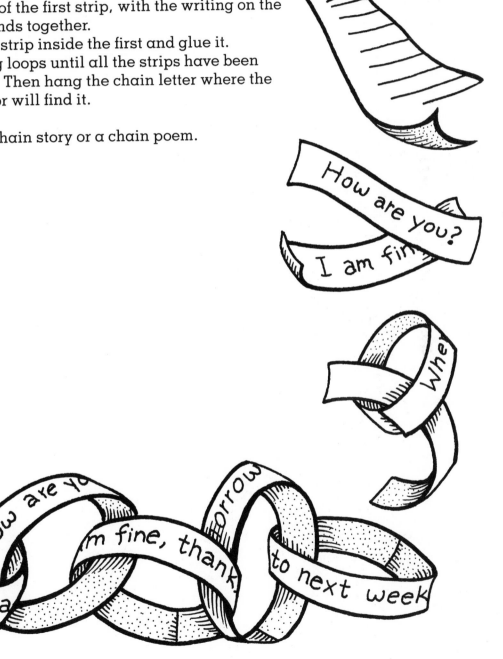

CLOTHES LINES

MATERIALS: paper, writing tools, wide masking tape

DIRECTIONS:
1. Think up one or more newsy sentences.
2. Print each sentence on a strip of wide masking tape.
3. Attach the tape to an article of clothing.

Variation: Some photocopy stores can convert words and simple drawings from plain paper to an iron-on transfer. The message can then be ironed onto a T-shirt or other garment.

COLOSSAL CARD

MATERIALS: paper, writing tools, butcher or construction paper, tape

DIRECTIONS:
1. On scratch paper, write the words for a giant-size greeting card.
2. Copy the words neatly on a large piece of butcher or construction paper. Try cutting the paper in a shape that fits the message.
3. Draw one or more pictures for added fun.
4. Tape the card in a place where it will be seen by the person it's for.

COSTUME CONVERSATIONS

MATERIALS: old sheets, scissors, markers, string, found objects as needed

DIRECTIONS:
1. Think up a character: for example, a robot, a superhero, a teacher, a doctor, a banker, or a police officer.
2. Use old sheets and other things to make the parts of the costume. For example, cut a cape for the superhero costume.
3. On the costume, write words that the character might say.

I'm a Halloween spirit
And I'm visiting you —
Please give me a treat
Or I'll have to say "Boo!"

I'm all electric,
Made of wires,
Nuts and bolts.
Give me candy
Or I'll give
you jolts!

CUE CARDS

MATERIALS: paper, writing tools, poster board

DIRECTIONS:
1. Write a script in which the audience plays a part by making sounds: for example, clapping, cheering, laughing, oohing and ahhing, stomping the feet, and whistling like the wind.
2. Print each direction in big letters on a large piece of poster board. This is called a "cue card." The cue card should be easy to read for someone sitting at the back of the theater.
3. Before the play begins, hold up each cue card so the audience can practice its part.
4. During the play, have someone hold up the cards at just the right moment.

Sample Script for Cue Card Play

First Pig:	Thanks for taking me in, Third Piggy. That Big Bad Wolf blew my house down and really scared me.
Second Pig:	The same thing happened to me.
Third Pig:	I'm glad you made it safely to my house.
First Pig:	Oh, no. Here comes the Big Bad Wolf.
Cue Card #1:	Ohhhhhhhhh!
Big Bad Wolf:	I'm going to huff and puff and blow your house down.
Cue Card #2:	Boooooooo!
Big Bad Wolf:	Well, what am I supposed to do, stop trying to catch the pigs?
Second Pig:	That would be great.
Cue Card #3:	Yeahhhh!
Big Bad Wolf:	And not blow the house down?
Third Pig:	We'd love that.
Cue Card #3:	Yeahhhh!
Big Bad Wolf:	And be nice to everybody?
Three Pigs:	That's what we want.
Cue Card #3:	Yeahhhh!
Big Bad Wolf:	OK. I'll give it a try.
Three Pigs:	Goody.
Big Bad Wolf:	That's the end of our little play.
Cue Card #4:	Clap your hands.

CUP COMPOSITION

MATERIALS: paper, writing tools, plain paper cup or plastic cup, plain self-sticking shelf paper

DIRECTIONS:
1. On scratch paper, work out a message that will fit around a drinking cup. The cup can be a gift for a friend or relative.
2. Cut a piece of shelf paper that will fit around the cup.
3. Use permanent markers to write the message onto the shelf paper. For interest, add a picture.
4. Attach the paper to the cup.

DESIGNER SIGN

MATERIALS: paper, writing tools, glue, hole punch, yarn, found objects

DIRECTIONS:
1. Find someone who needs a sign, for example, a shop owner.
2. On a piece of construction paper or cardboard use a pencil to write the message, for example, "Open" or "Do not disturb."
3. Find material to letter the sign with. For example, a sign for a sewing store could be lettered with buttons. A sign for someone who likes to eat popcorn might be lettered with popcorn.
4. Glue the lettering material to the sign.
5. Punch a hole in the top corners.
6. Run a piece of yarn through the holes to hang the sign.

DOORBELL DO'S AND DON'TS

MATERIALS: construction paper, writing tools, scissors, clear self-sticking shelf paper or plastic wrap (optional), glue or tape

DIRECTIONS:
1. Cut a hole in a square or circular piece of paper so that the paper will make a frame around a doorbell.
2. On the paper, write a set of rules for people who might ring the doorbell.
3. If the doorbell is exposed to the weather, cover the rules with shelf paper or plastic wrap.
4. Glue or tape the rules in place.

Before ringing, please read:

1. Please ring only twice.

2. If you are selling, please go to the next house.

DOORKNOB DISPATCH

MATERIALS: paper, writing tools, doorknob dispatch pattern, poster board

DIRECTIONS:
1. Think up two messages that belong on someone's doorknob.
2. Trace or photocopy the doorknob dispatch pattern (next page). Use the pattern to cut out a doorknob dispatch hangup.
3. Write a message on each side of the doorknob dispatch. A picture can add interest.

Variation: Make a doorknob dispatch for a famous person or for a make-believe character.

FACT-FINDING FLYER

MATERIALS: construction paper, writing tools, envelope, string, pad of paper, stapler

DIRECTIONS:
1. Think up a question that needs an answer. Write the question on the construction paper.
2. Write the words "Put your answer here" on the envelope.
3. Staple the answer envelope to the construction paper.
4. Staple or tie one end of the string to a pen. Staple the other end of the string to the poster.
5. Staple the pad of paper to the poster.
6. Put the poster where many people might see it.
7. Check the envelope regularly to see if the question has been answered.
8. Later, report the findings on the bulletin board.

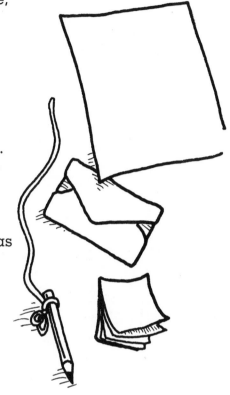

FLAGGED FACTS

MATERIALS: paper, writing tools, construction paper or cloth, wooden dowels, thumbtacks or stapler

DIRECTIONS:
1. Write about five or ten short facts about one subject.
2. Cut out one paper or cloth flag for each fact.
3. Print each fact on a separate paper or cloth flag.
4. Use staples or thumbtacks to attach each flag to a wooden dowel.
5. Give each flag to a marcher and have a flag parade.

FRAME-UP

MATERIALS: light-colored construction paper, writing tools, photo or other picture, scissors, tape

DIRECTIONS:
1. Find a picture to frame: for example, a family snapshot, a school photo, or a picture clipped from a newspaper or magazine.
2. On scratch paper, write a few sentences that tell something interesting about the picture: for example, who's in it, where it is, or what's going on.
3. Place the picture on the construction paper. With a pencil, lightly trace around the picture.
4. Cut out a window for the picture, but make it smaller than the space outlined with the pencil.
5. Tape the picture so that it faces out through the window.
6. Write all around the picture, so the words make a border.

My dog Spice

can catch a Frisbee better than I can. However, I can throw it better than she can.

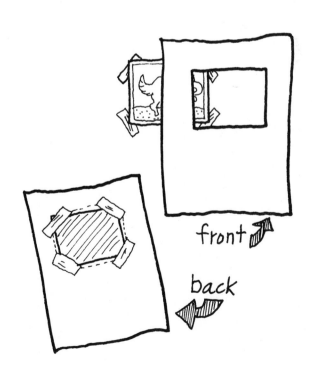

front

back

HOLIDAY HANGUP

MATERIALS: paper, writing tools, paper plate, glue, pine needles or glitter, hole punch, yarn, thumbtack or tape

DIRECTIONS:
1. Write a holiday greeting that is short enough to fit in the inner circle of the paper plate.
2. Copy the message on the plate.
3. Put glue around the edge of the plate. Then sprinkle on pine needles or glitter.
4. Above the words punch a hole near the edge of the plate.
5. String a piece of yarn through the hole.
6. Use a thumbtack or tape to hang the plate on a door.

Welcome to our home.

May this holiday season bring you joy!
The Smith Family

LITTER LITERATURE

MATERIALS: construction paper, writing tools, tape, clear self-sticking shelf paper

DIRECTIONS:
1. Think about why some people toss their trash onto the ground instead of into a trash can or wastebasket.
2. On scratch paper, write a few words or a poem that might teach people not to litter.
3. Copy the words onto the construction paper. To make the poster eye-catching, add a picture.
4. If the sign is for an outside can, cover it with clear shelf paper.
5. Tape the poster to a trash can or wastebasket.
6. Watch to see if people begin to use the can or basket.

LIVELY LABELS

MATERIALS: empty tin cans and plastic bottles, paper, writing tools, glue

DIRECTIONS:
1. Remove the label from the container.
2. Cut out a new label that matches the size of the old one.
3. Write a new name for the product.
4. Write a message that tells about the product. The words can be serious or silly.
5. Glue the new label to the container.
6. Make a display of containers with homemade labels.

MAP CAP

MATERIALS: paper, writing tools, atlas

DIRECTIONS:
1. Fold the paper into a hat.
2. On one side, draw the map of an important place: for example, a place in the news.
3. On the other side, write a few words that tell why the place is important.
4. Wear the cap and be ready to tell people about the place.

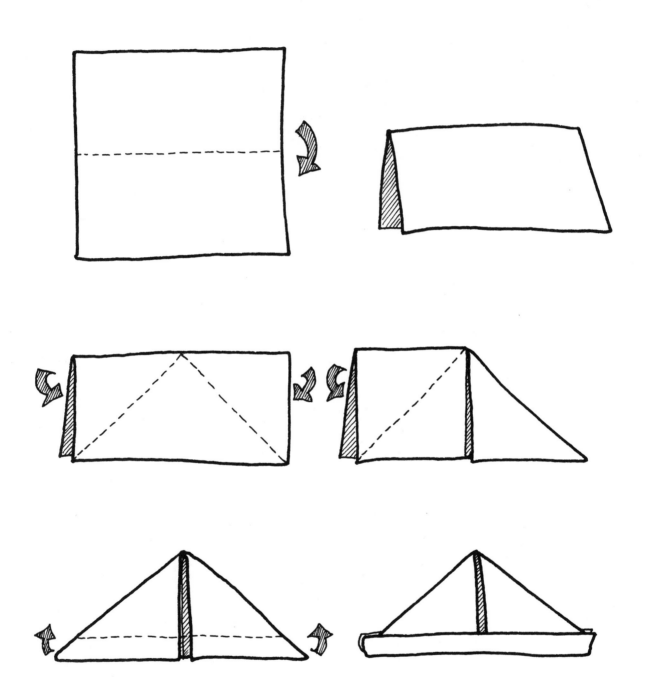

MAP REPORT

MATERIALS: paper, writing tools, atlas or map, clear self-sticking shelf paper, tape

DIRECTIONS:
1. Draw or get a map of a country or of the world.
2. Cover the map with shelf paper to protect it.
3. From the newspaper, TV, or radio, collect stories about places in the news.
4. Write the news on a piece of paper, and tape it to its place on the map.
5. From time to time, take down the old news and put up new news.

Variation: Fill up the map with personal news: for example, "The cereal I eat for breakfast comes from Battle Creek, Michigan."

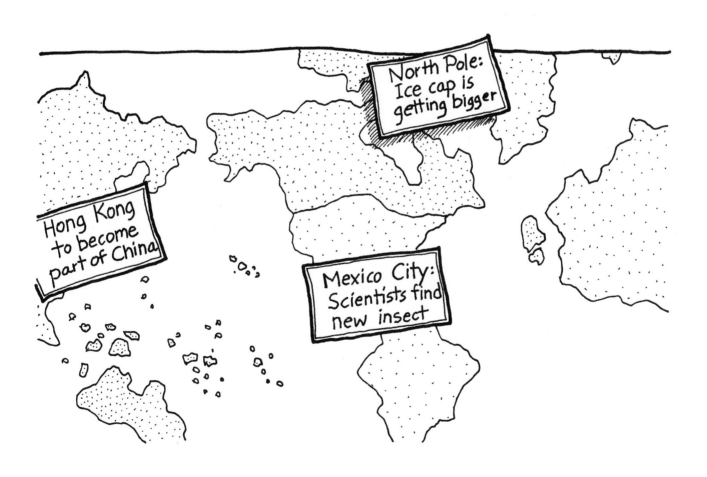

Alaska

Canada

United States

Australia

MESSAGE BOARD

MATERIALS: construction paper, writing tools, bulletin board, envelope or small box, string, tape, stapler, thumbtacks

DIRECTIONS:
1. Find an empty bulletin board that many people go by.
2. Make a sign that invites people to leave messages. Tell how long the messages will be left up.
3. Make a holder for paper that people can use to write notes. Attach the holder with staples, tape, or thumbtacks.
4. Use a stapler to attach a pencil to the string and the string to the board.
5. Check the board from time to time to make sure old messages are removed. Also make sure that there is paper in the paper holder and that the pencil is still there.

MOBILE MASTERPIECE

MATERIALS: construction paper, writing tools, hole punch, yarn, wire hangers

DIRECTIONS:
1. Think up pairs of opposites: for example, *up/down*, *slow/fast*, and *heavy/light*.
2. Cut out pairs of shapes from construction paper: for example, two circles, two squares, and two triangles.
3. Write an opposite in each cutout.
4. Punch holes in the shapes.
5. Use equal lengths of yarn to tie each word pair to a hanger.

Variation: Instead of opposites, use rhyming words (*hear/near*), anagrams (*spot/tops*), reversible words (*ton/not*), or other word pairs.

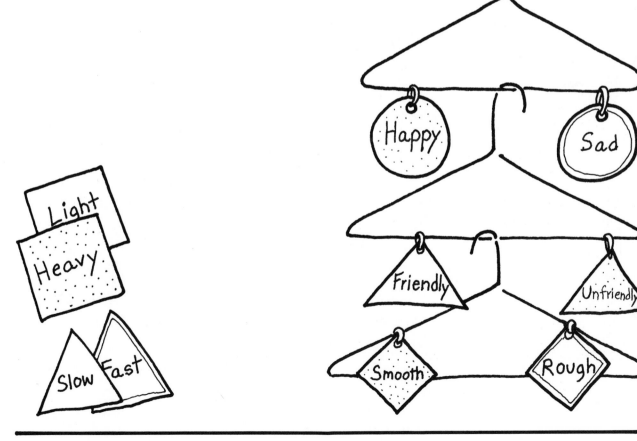

MUSEUM MEMO

MATERIALS: paper or cards, writing tools, something to display

DIRECTIONS:
1. Create a display. A display might be drawings, photographs, a rock or stamp collection, a set of baseball cards, tools used in a hobby, or whatever.
2. Think up questions people might have about the display.
3. On a piece of paper or on several small cards, write a few sentences or paragraphs that answer the questions. This writing should help viewers learn more from the display and enjoy it more, too.
4. For extra interest, add pictures.

PLANTED WORDS

MATERIALS: paper, writing tools, index card, plant, popsicle stick, stapler, flowerpot

DIRECTIONS:
1. Get a potted plant. Find out about the plant by reading a book or talking to someone who knows about it.
2. Write a paragraph or a poem about the plant. Then copy the writing onto an index card.
3. Staple the index card onto a popsicle stick.
4. Push the stick into the flowerpot.

Variation: Draw or cut out a picture of a real or imaginary plant, plant the picture, and then write about it.

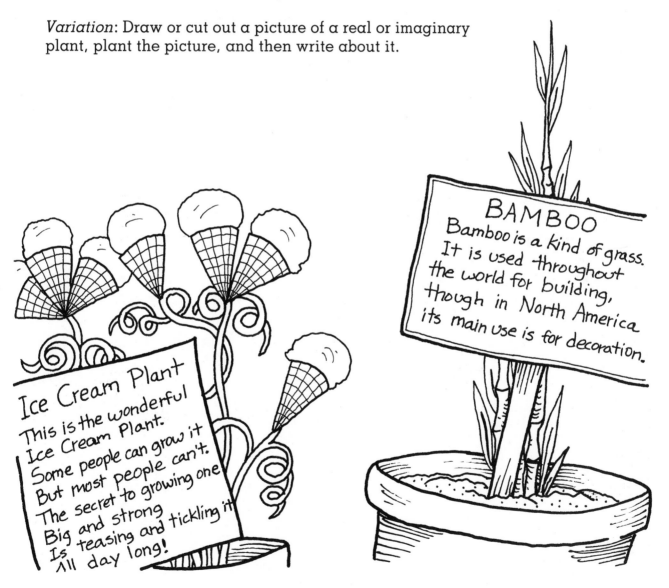

Ice Cream Plant
This is the wonderful
Ice Cream Plant.
Some people can grow it
But most people can't.
The secret to growing one
Big and strong
Is teasing and tickling it
All day long!

BAMBOO
Bamboo is a kind of grass.
It is used throughout
the world for building,
though in North America
its main use is for decoration.

PLAQUE FACTS

MATERIALS: construction paper, writing tools, scissors

DIRECTIONS:
1. Find a place of interest: for example, the oldest store in town. Ask the person in charge if he or she would be willing to put up a poster "plaque" that tells about the place.
2. If the answer is yes, write a story about the place.
3. Copy the story onto a piece of construction paper. For extra interest, cut the paper in a shape that fits the story.
4. Get permission to hang the poster.

POSTED POETRY

MATERIALS: paper, writing tools, tagboard, thumbtacks, flat sticks for posts

DIRECTIONS:
1. Write a four-line poem. Lines two and four should rhyme. Each line should have five or fewer words.
2. Write each line on a separate piece of tagboard.
3. Fasten the tagboard to a post with thumbtacks.
4. Post each line of the poem in a place where people will walk or drive by.

PROJECTOR PRESENTATION

MATERIALS: paper, writing tools, overhead projector transparency, felt-tip marker with washable ink, overhead projector

DIRECTIONS:
1. Create a short piece of writing: for example, a poem, short-short story, poster, or song lyric.
2. Copy the writing onto the transparency. Add a border.
3. Use the projector to share the writing with a big group.

QUOTE FLOAT

MATERIALS: construction paper, writing tools, hole punch, yarn

DIRECTIONS:
1. Find a short quotation to share. Take it from a famous story or a song. Or make it up from scratch.
2. Print the quotation on the construction paper.
3. Punch holes in the top two corners of the paper.
4. Hang the float where everyone can see it.

To have a friend, be one.
Ralph Waldo Emerson

Sentence of the week
by Joellen Frazer

The scared snake rolled itself up like a hose.

I like it this way.

ROLL-DOWN RIDDLE

MATERIALS: paper, writing tools, hole punch, window shade, yarn, tape

DIRECTIONS:
1. Find or make up a riddle.
2. Write the question on a piece of paper: for example, "How does a baby ghost cry?" Underneath the question, write the words: "Pull down for the answer."
3. Punch holes in the top corners of the question sheet, and attach it to the ring pull of the shade with a piece of yarn.
4. Write the answer—in this case, "Boo-hoo! Boo-hoo!" on another piece of paper.
5. Tape the answer onto the shade, and roll the shade up.

Variation: Instead of a riddle, ask a quiz-show or school question.

answer inside

How many people played in the world's largest game of musical chairs?

(Pull down for the answer)

RULES AND REGULATIONS

MATERIALS: paper, writing tools, construction paper, tape or stapler

DIRECTIONS:

1. Find a place that needs a list of rules: for example, the school library, a clubhouse, or the kitchen at home. It could even be a make-believe place: for example, the home of the witch in *Hansel and Gretel*.
2. On a piece of scratch paper, practice writing out the rules. This will include thinking up a title for the rules poster and also putting the rules in order.
3. Copy the rules neatly onto a piece of construction paper. For extra interest, add a picture.
4. Use tape or a stapler to post the rules.

Places that could use a list of real or pretend rules and regulations:

Band room
Bathroom
Bedroom
Bus
Cafeteria
Cage of wild animals
Classroom
Garden
Gymnasium
Hallway

Kitchen
Library
Movie theater
Park
Playground
Space station
Stores around town
Swimming pool
TV watching area
Workshop

Rules for Saucer Crew:

SANDWICH BOARD BLARNEY

MATERIALS: paper, writing tools, construction paper, hole punch, string

DIRECTIONS:
1. Think up a message that people need to see right away. It could announce a backyard puppet show or a band concert or a fundraising drive.
2. Practice writing the message on scratch paper until it's clear.
3. Print the message lightly in pencil on a piece of construction paper. When the spacing is right, go over the letters in ink or crayon. Then print the same message—or a similar one—on another piece of construction paper.
4. Add pictures to build interest.
5. Punch holes in the top corners of each poster.
6. Connect the top left holes with one string, and the top right holes with another string of equal length. Make the strings long enough so that a person can wear the two posters like a vest.

Come to the rock display in the library.

You'll see many beautiful rocks, plus interesting books about rock collecting.

SHAPE REPORT

MATERIALS: paper, writing tools, construction paper, scissors, hole punch and yarn or tape

DIRECTIONS:
1. Pick an object to tell about: for example, a toy, a kind of food, or something used at school.
2. On scratch paper, write a story, a poem, or a report about the thing. If necessary, read about the thing or ask someone about it before writing.
3. Draw a big picture of the thing on the construction paper. Make the picture big enough so the writing will fit in it.
4. Cut out the shape.
5. Print the story, report, or poem onto the shape.
6. Punch a hole in the top of the poster and hang with yarn, or use tape to put it up.

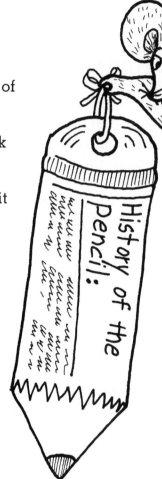

SLIDE SHOW

MATERIALS: paper, writing tools, unwanted slides, dish, bleach, fine-tip felt marker with washable ink, slide projector

DIRECTIONS:
1. Put about ten unwanted 35 mm slides in order so that they tell a story.
2. Write two or three sentences for each slide. This will be the slide-show script and will be read aloud during the show.
3. Prepare a set of blank slides by soaking unwanted slides in a dish of bleach. (Blank slides can also be purchased at a photo store.)
4. On each blank slide, use the marker to write a single word that will introduce the next picture slide in the story. For example, if the first picture slide shows a house, the first title slide might read "Home."
5. As the slides are presented to the audience, read the script aloud. For more interest, play background music.

SPECIAL DELIVERY MAILBOX

MATERIALS: paper, writing tools, large manila envelope, tape or string

DIRECTIONS:

1. Think about a subject that would be interesting to read about.
2. Write a note asking for letters about that subject. For interest, add a picture.
3. Tape the note to a large envelope.
4. Use tape or string to post the mail pouch in a place where many people will see it.
5. Be sure to answer the mail that gets put into the pouch.

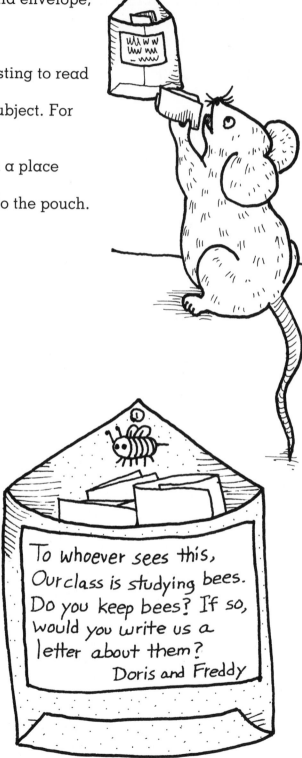

Do you have any good cookie recipes? Please share them with us for our school bake sale.

To whoever sees this, Our class is studying bees. Do you keep bees? If so, would you write us a letter about them?
Doris and Freddy

STORY ART

MATERIALS: drawing paper, writing tools, drawing tools

DIRECTIONS:
1. Think up a picture that tells a story.
2. Draw the picture using about half of the paper.
3. Write about the story in the space next to or under the picture. Be sure to include a title.

TALKY TAPESTRY

MATERIALS: construction paper, writing tools, drawing tools

DIRECTIONS:
1. Pick a true or a make-believe story. It could be about a trip, a dream, or characters in a fairy tale.
2. On several sheets of scratch paper, sketch the main scenes from the story.
3. Lightly in pencil, copy the scenes onto large pieces of construction paper. Then go over the sketch with colored pens or crayons.
4. Over, under, or next to the picture of each scene, write words that help explain what's going on.
5. Mount the scenes on a bulletin board or a wall.

WALKING-TOUR WRITE-UP

MATERIALS: paper, writing tools, index cards, tape

DIRECTIONS:
1. Find a place that people might like to visit: for example, the school, a park, an area of town, or even a house.
2. List each stop of the tour: for example, a tour of a garden might include stops at different flower plots, vegetable plots, fruit trees, and so on.
3. Put the stops in order.
4. On small or large index cards, write a paragraph or two about each stop. Start with the name of the place. Then tell the reader an interesting fact or what to look for. End by telling the reader where to go next.
5. Attach each write-up in a place where it can easily be seen.
6. Make sure people hear about the walking tour: for example, by sending news about it to a local newspaper, or by putting up announcements.

School
Walking Tour
Stop 3: Library

Shhh. You are about to enter the library. It was started by Mrs. Lake.

When you leave, turn left and go to Room 122. That is Stop 4.

Shhh!

WELCOMING WORDS

MATERIALS: construction paper, writing tools, scissors

DIRECTIONS:
1. Find a doorway that needs a welcome sign.
2. On scratch paper, write a message that says something important about the place to be entered.
3. Cut a piece of construction paper that will fit the space above the door.
4. Copy the words onto the construction paper. Make the letters big enough so they can easily be read by people passing below the sign.
5. Add a picture for interest.

WINDOW WEEKLY

MATERIALS: paper, writing tools, construction paper, tape

DIRECTIONS:

1. Get permission to use a store window that lots of people go by.

2. Prepare a poster newspaper that will interest people who walk by the window. The paper could give news: for example, something that has happened in town. Or it could present interesting lessons from school.

3. Tape the display to the inside of the window.

4. Change the display every week.

YARN YARN

MATERIALS: paper, writing tools, hole punch, pictures from magazines and newspapers (optional), glue, yarn, scissors

DIRECTIONS:
1. Make up a story or a joke that can be broken into several parts or scenes.
2. Write each part on a separate piece of paper.
3. Illustrate each part with an original or found picture.
4. Punch a hole near the top two corners of each sheet.
5. String a long piece of yarn for hanging up the story.
6. Use two equal lengths of yarn to attach each page of the story to the long piece of yarn.

RESOURCES

Art Tips

1. Make a sketch on scratch paper. It's OK to get ideas from books or objects.
2. When drawing the picture on the actual poster, first try it lightly in pencil
3. Check to make sure the picture is big enough.
4. Finally, go over your drawing in ink or crayon. Then carefully erase the pencil lines.

Borders

Use interesting-looking borders to make posters more eye-catching.

Woven yarn

Stick-on stars

cut fringe

Glued-on pictures

Lettering Tips

For poster headlines, try inventing letters from materials that relate to the subject of the poster. Some examples:

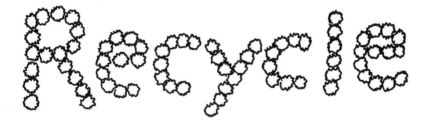

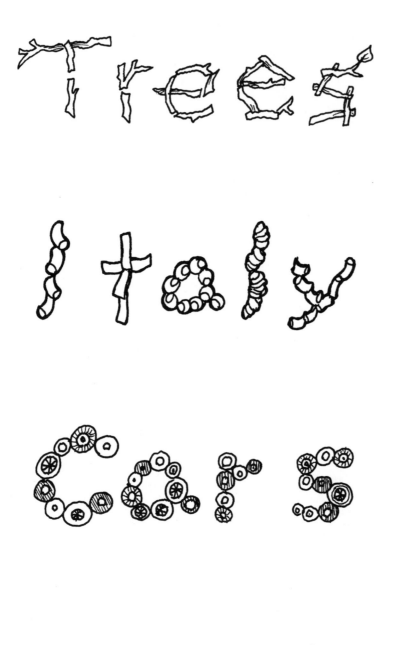

Trees

Italy

Cars

Hobbies

Patterns

Use the following pictures for ideas to illustrate hangups.

These buttons may

machine.

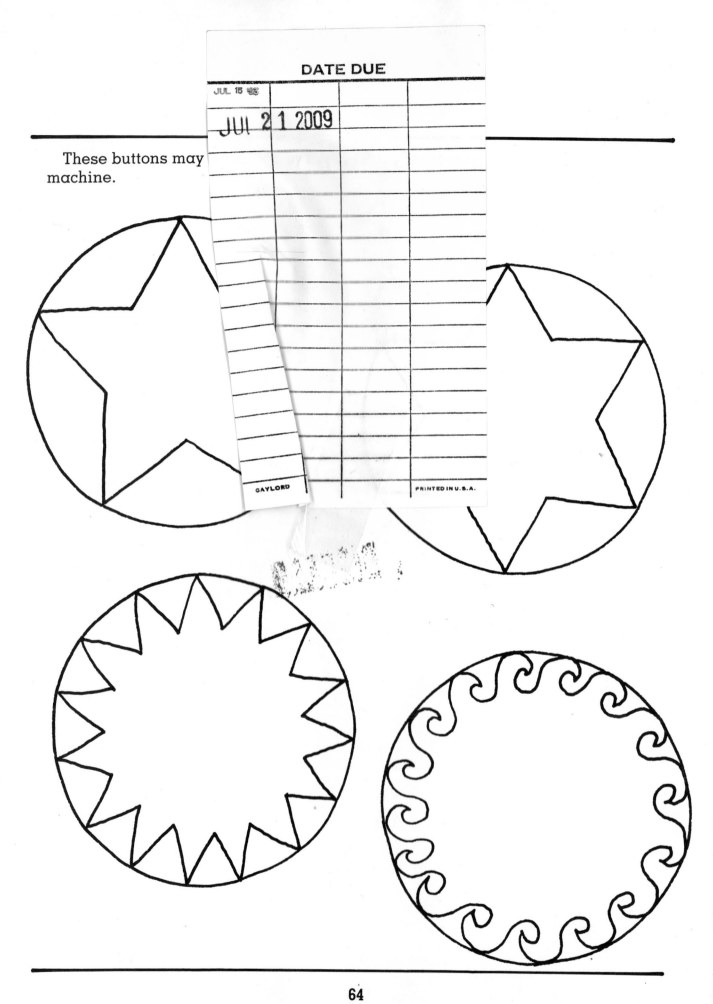